YUM TUM,
WE GET IT DONE!

By

Melanie Stewart

Partner book for
YUM TUM, GOOD FOOD IS FUN!
and
YUM TUM, FOR DAD AND MUM!

Disclaimer: This information is in no way intended to diagnose or treat specific medical conditions. It contains basic information, that is publicly available, and includes generic information about food, food preparation, nutrient data, physiological mechanisms of action or interaction. It is not intended as individualized advice and any suggestions I make are not a substitute for you own personal research. As always, do not discontinue any medications without your doctor's consent.

Your brain is the way
that you think what you thought
about all of the things
that you know,
or know not.

YOUR STOMACH GROWLS BACK IN reply (THAT'S HIS greetiN')

AND it RUMBLES and GRUMBLES UNTIL YOU HAVE eaten.

WELL, LET'S FIND OUT!
WOULD YOU LIKE TO MEET
THE REST OF THE ORGANS
WHO WORK WHEN YOU EAT?

Like a train on a track,
With a big job to do,
The way things work best
is to chew-chew, chew-chew!

And what I love most
while I'm chewing away
is to taste all the food
that you eat in a day!

Each time you SWALLOW your Food takes a ride doWN your "eSOPHAGUS", a SLippery tube SLide.

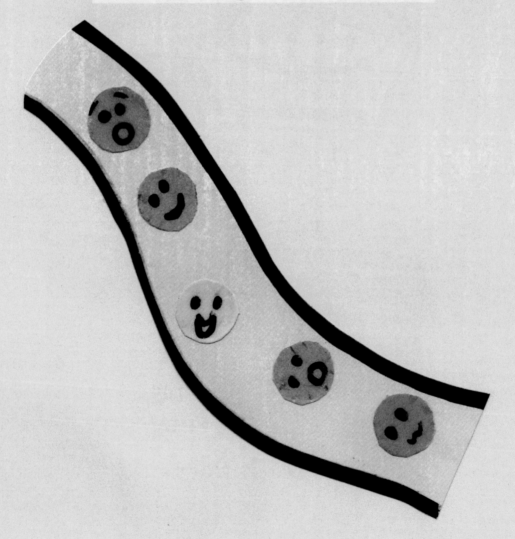

AND then it MOVeS ON to your SMall intestine-

I extract all the good things, that's What I'M best iN!

ALL OF the NUtrieNtS, thiNGS With great poWer, I FiNd and absorb theM For you by the HOUr!

The cells in your body
Well, they make you, YOU!

Your brain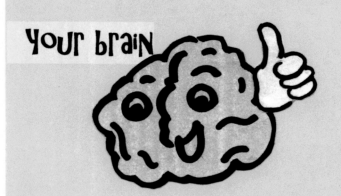

and your heart

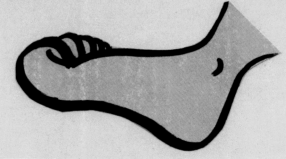

and the foot in your shoe!

Cells need all the nutrients
that you consume
For power to play, learn,
or clean up your room.

It's quite a LONG JOURNEY but, it's NOT doNe yet.
There is oNe MOre organ it's time that you
Met.

I aM your COLON,
I LiKe Fiber rich Food
To help Keep Me cLean
AND HeaLTHy and good!

My job is important!
I process things last...

I don't like to be S L O W

(constipation)

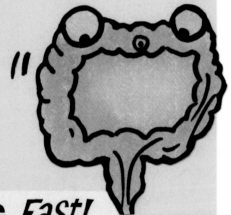

I don't like to be *Fast!*

(diarrhea)

THe jouRNey iS oveR,
We've come to tHe eNd.

OuR Food HaS beeN pRoceSSed
TiLL We eat agaiN.

And then the food leaves right out of your tushie—
your fanny, your bottom,
with one little pushie.

Made in the USA
San Bernardino, CA
15 May 2016